Daniel Schnyder

CROSSING OVER
Essentials for Jazz and Classical Flute

An exploration of modern compositional devices and their interaction with jazz harmony and phrasing

T0166263

SECOND FLOOR MUSIC

EXCLUSIVELY DISTRIBUTED BY

HAL•LEONARD®
CORPORATION

7777 W. BLUEMOUND RD. P.O. BOX 13819 MILWAUKEE, WI 53213

Etudes and Exercises by **Daniel Schnyder**

Edited by **Rob Hardt**

Diagrams by **Rob Hardt** and **Osho Endo**

Book and cover design by **Terry Chamberlain**

Music typography by **Osho Endo**

Photographs of Daniel Schnyder and Thomas Chapin by **Thomas Cugini**

Cover photograph by **Terry Chamberlain**

Biography of Daniel Schnyder by **Steve Lambert**

A DON SICKLER PRODUCTION

SECOND FLOOR MUSIC, 130 West 28th Street, New York, NY 10001 USA

http://www.secondfloormusic.com

Daniel Schnyder

CROSSING OVER

Essentials for Jazz and Classical Flute

An exploration of modern compositional devices and their interaction with jazz harmony and phrasing

SECOND FLOOR MUSIC

This book is dedicated to the memory of Thomas Chapin

March 9, 1957 - February 13, 1998

Foreword

Melodic material used in most jazz music today falls into one of two categories: diatonic material that composers have been exploring for over 300 years; or attempts at more modern esoteric devices such as twelve tone rows or motivic cells, often resulting in neither artistic nor popular success. There exists, however, a middle ground that, while transcending diatonic music, still possesses a comprehensive, internal logic that makes it challenging for a skilled musician to play, yet pleasant to hear.

This book concentrates on that middle ground. There are five sets of exercises that explore the musical language that emerges from combining different triads and 4-note chords that do not occur together in Western tonal music but nonetheless have much in common, thereby creating new and interesting sounds when used together. These exercises also explore new scales that emerge from taking predetermined sets of selected intervals and organically extending them into a new scale that, while not fitting comfortably within the realm of traditional Western music, has a unique sound that works well in jazz or a modern classical setting.

Schnyder then goes one step further by using the melodic material developed in these exercises to create a very musical set of etudes. By using the material in moderation, maintaining variety, and being sensitive to the natural tendencies of the music rather than imposing a rigid theoretical approach, he strikes an appropriate balance of theory and intuition. The etudes sound fresh and uncontrived, yet the references to the theoretical foundation are clear. References to the exercise that a phrase comes from appear wherever applicable.

This book is perfect for the jazz musician looking to expand his vocabulary without alienating the listener. It will also be of great interest for the classical musician looking for new, unexplored musical landscapes. Regardless of the nature of your musical background, however, you will surely find this book both challenging and very rewarding.

Rob Hardt, editor

Preface

Crossing Over: Essentials For Jazz And Classical Flute concentrates on symmetric, chromatic and expanded diatonic or pentatonic concepts. Furthermore, the etudes with chord symbols also emphasize the interaction between the melody and the underlying harmonic structure. You can hear the music one-dimensionally and focus only on its horizontal development, or you can hear the etudes with chord changes two-dimensionally, which means you follow the relationship of the horizontal (i.e., the line or melody) and vertical information (the chords) simultaneously. One can compare this to the different approaches to music of Ornette Coleman on one hand and Clifford Brown or Charlie Parker on the other.

The purpose of this study, then, is to show you ways not only to develop your technique and phrasing, and your feeling for more freedom in jazz improvisation over chord changes, but also to expand your musical knowledge and experience, which may lead to new creative ideas in the fields of composition and arrangement.

The greatest benefit to the classical musician lies in the exposure to new compositional devices which will lead to greater facility and comfort in unusual tonal frameworks. A jazz musician will also benefit from this exposure because the inclusion of chord symbols in many of the etudes allows one to clearly discern how these new devices can be practically and musically integrated into improvised solos.

The instrumental process you are going through by playing these exercises and etudes is actually a true compositional process. You put small things (intervals, triads, scale fragments, etc.) that are already known to you together and finally end up with your own creations. The process is not unlike molecular chemistry where you build a specific polymer out of a finite number of known elements. But please, don't take an overly rigid or mathematical approach to these etudes and exercises, but instead enjoy the new material and explore it in a childlike way. Fool around with the information, play the exercises by heart and explore their surroundings freely.

Performance Notes

When playing the etudes, keep in mind that the indicated phrasing represents just one solution. There are other possibilities (more or less tonguing) depending on the tempo and your technical abilities.

As in baroque music, most jazz-related music requires the player to come up with his or her own concept of dynamics (gradations of loudness and softness) in performance. However, I have included dynamics markings in all but two etudes. Those two etudes have dynamic indications in parentheses (*mf*). In creating your own interpretations, there are certain rules:
- The highest note in a phrase is stressed.
- The notes immediately before the highest note in a phrase are slightly suppressed.
- Tongued notes are louder than slurred notes.

Jazz music has, like baroque music, a dynamic microstructure[1], while romantic music has basically a dynamic macrostructure[2], and classical music, if well-played, has both. The dynamic markings, then, provide you with a macrostructure, but the microstructure is up to you, the performer, but should be informed by the concepts set forth here.

In order to achieve the right phrasing, it is important not to interrupt or alter the basic airstream. Despite the dynamic microstructure mentioned before, the airstream must remain constantly the same. All dynamic alterations are made by the tongue that holds, releases, or partially withholds the airstream. The alteration of the airstream with the tongue gives jazz phrasing its unique "talking" quality. Notes that are fingered but totally suppressed because of an upcoming peak are called "ghost notes."

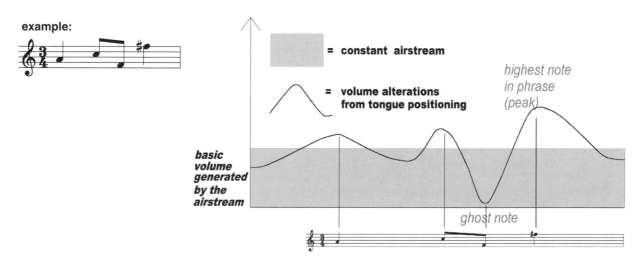

example:

= constant airstream

= volume alterations from tongue positioning

highest note in phrase (peak)

basic volume generated by the airstream

ghost note

1. A structure in which the dynamics change gradually from note to note.
2. A structure in which the dynamics change gradually within sections.

ETUDES

These etudes are designed for the advanced jazz player as well as for the classical musician. All etudes can be played and performed as solo pieces. In addition, the etudes with chord symbols can be performed with keyboard or jazz rhythm section accompaniment.

Roman numerals beneath the staff refer you to the exercise section (pages 23 to 43). Some of the specific technical problems and musical ideas which are unfamiliar to most of us are presented there in a condensed, theoretical way.

You may vary the phrasing and articulation depending on the tempo. The final tempo shown (e.g., ♩ = 84 - 120) may look unrealistic at first, however, as soon as you understand the structures and fractals[1] within the patterns that make up the lines, fast tempos will become much easier.

1. A fractal, as the term is used in this book, is a small melodic fragment (an interval, triad, scale or scale fragment) which serves as a building block.

The Shepherd Of The Galaxis

DANIEL SCHNYDER

* Press rim of key down without covering the key hole. This is the mirror note of the scale. [see IV 7]

Dark Matter

DANIEL SCHNYDER

Argon

DANIEL SCHNYDER

Uptempo Latin (♩ = *ca.* 96-132)

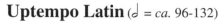

Big Crunch

DANIEL SCHNYDER

Big Chill

DANIEL SCHNYDER

Anima

DANIEL SCHNYDER

Rumor

Medium swing (♩ = *ca.* 144-168)

DANIEL SCHNYDER

Chromata

DANIEL SCHNYDER

EXERCISES

These exercises combine known musical fractals (intervals, triads, scales) in a "new" way, somehow making the known unknown. All the fractals individually are very easy for the mind and the fingers. However, the combination and superimposition of these fractals may result in a new and difficult pattern for your ears and fingers, which is at the same time pleasant and familiar for the amateur or unschooled listener who hears it superficially and relates it instantly to the known fractal structure.

The exercises shown here are merely representative selections from an almost infinite realm of possibilities. Once you understand the structure of a particular exercise, it will be easy for you to expand upon it in any way you choose and even come up with your own creations. Furthermore, the range of any exercise can be extended by adding notes according to the underlying fractal principle. The pattern of intervals is indicated at the beginning of an exercise (e.g., ‖: 1-1-1-1½ :‖). As each line is transposed, the interval from the original starting note is shown as +½ , +1, +1½ , and so on. Wherever you do not see a repetition sign, the pattern is derived from a constantly growing or shrinking fractal (see the graphic examples on the following page).

As in the etudes, patterns reappear in many different mutations. The succession of notes within a structure can always be altered and adapted to the musical needs at hand.

The following graphic examples may aid visualization of the general shape of linear and non-linear patterns. Note that the distinction between "linear" and "non-linear" was made because of technical, musical reasons, not mathematical considerations. It feels fundamentally different whether a pattern repeats itself in the octave (**I**) or not (**II**). The rule is, if the interval steps of your pattern added together results in the numbers ½, 1, 1½, 2, 3 or 6, it is a "linear" pattern; if not, it is a "non-linear" pattern. The family of linear patterns is finite; the family of non-linear patterns is infinite and only limited by practical and musical considerations.

linear patterns

I. 2 (page 24)

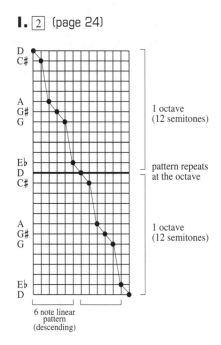

non-linear patterns

II. 1 (page 28)

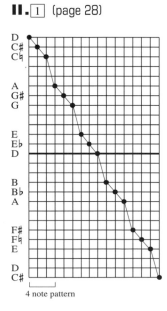

II. 10 (page 32)

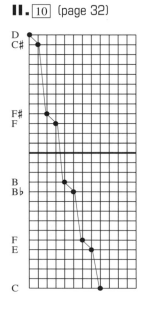

II. 11 (page 33)

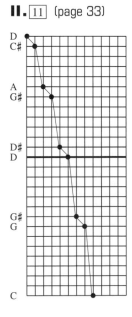

I. linear patterns

patterns that repeat at the octave

‖: ½–½–1 :‖

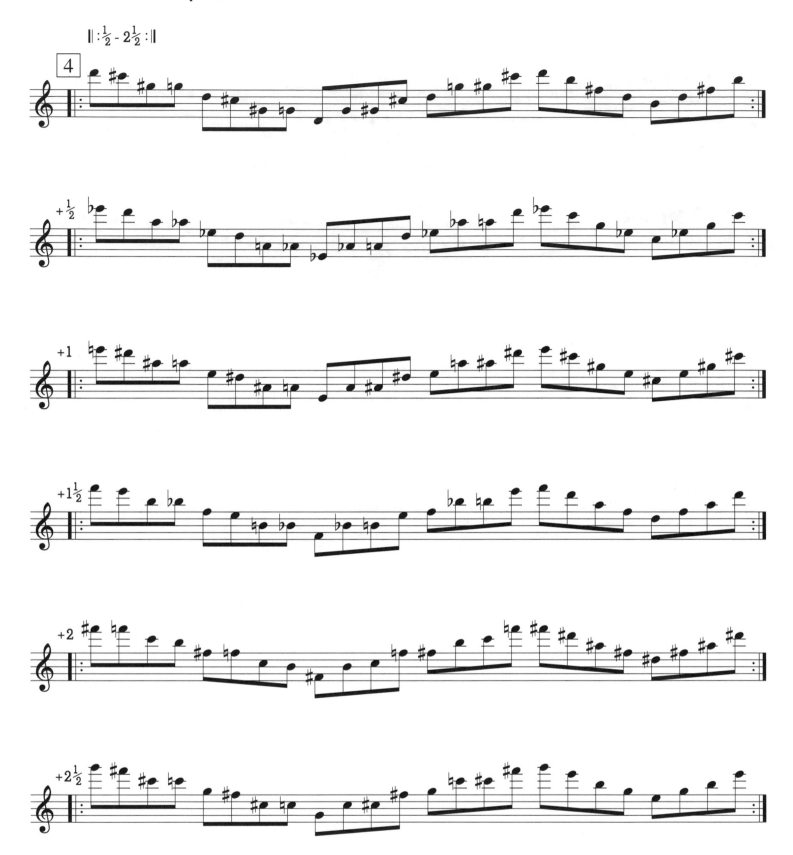

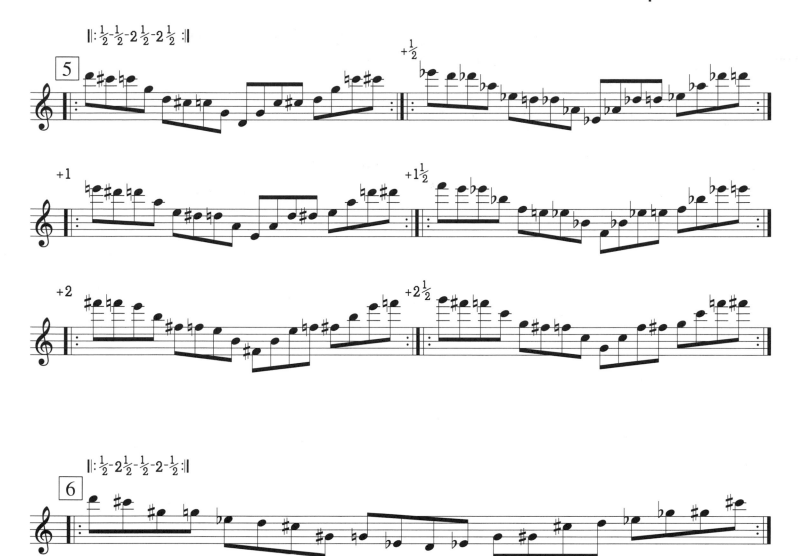

7

This family also includes: diminished scales

whole tone scales

diminished seventh chords

tritones

II. non-linear patterns

structures that do not repeat at the octave

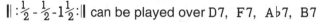

1

2

II. non-linear patterns

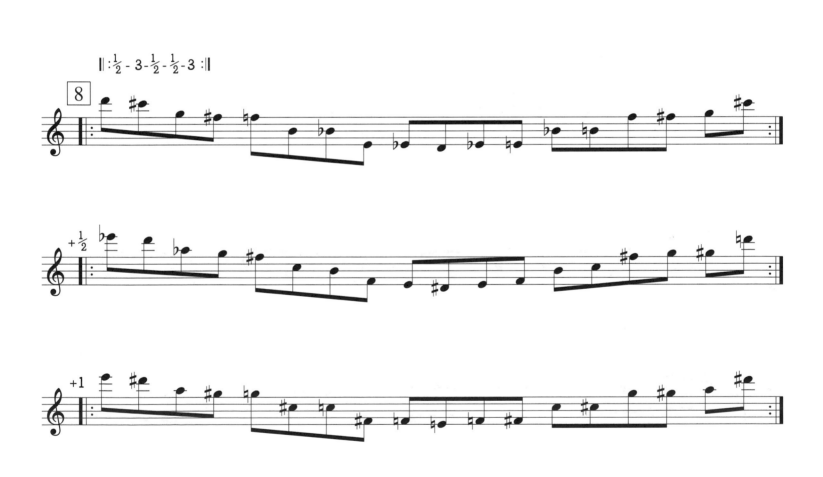

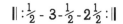

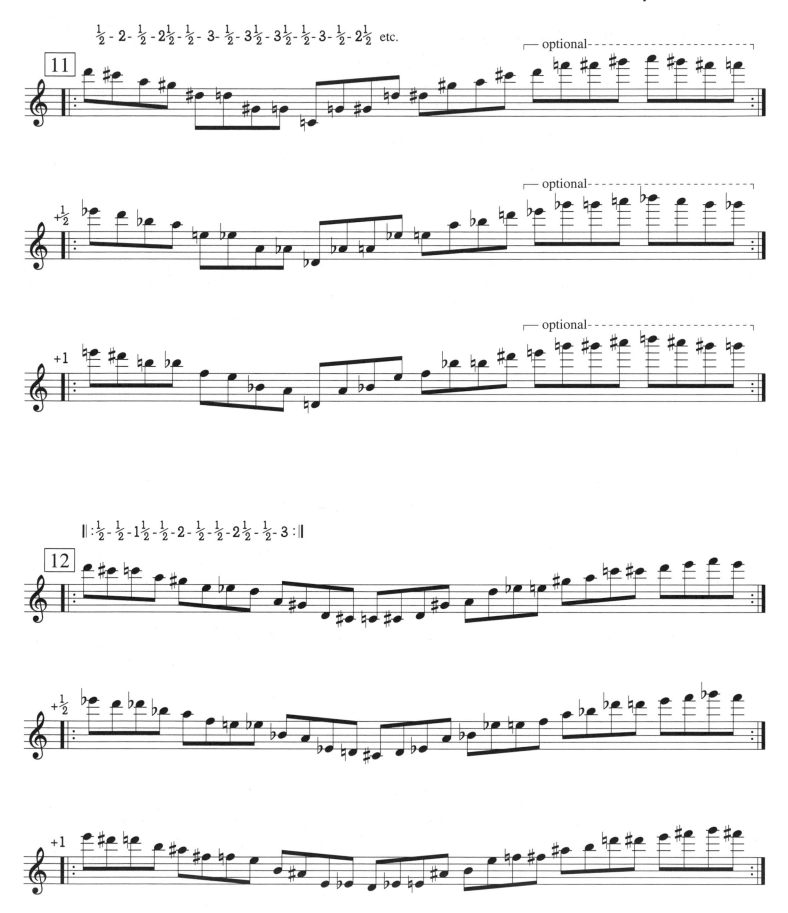

This family can be expanded and mutated *ad lib.*

IIIa. composed patterns (triads)

patterns made out of the transposition of the same chord

major triads, ascending and descending in half-steps

1

└── 2nd inv. ┘ └ 1st inv. ┘

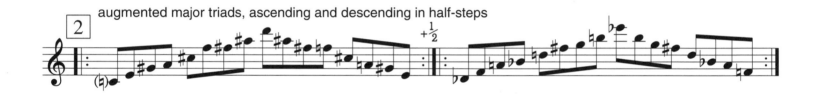

augmented major triads, ascending and descending in half-steps

2

"sus4" triads, ascending and descending in half-steps

3

diminished triads, ascending and descending in half-steps

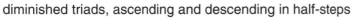

diminished triads, ascending and descending in whole-steps

minor triads, ascending and descending in half-steps

minor triads, ascending and descending in half-steps

pentatonic scales, ascending and descending in half-steps

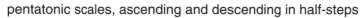

pentatonic scales, ascending and descending in half-steps

9

+½

+1

+1½

IIIb. composed patterns (scales)

structures derived from the transposition of scale fragments

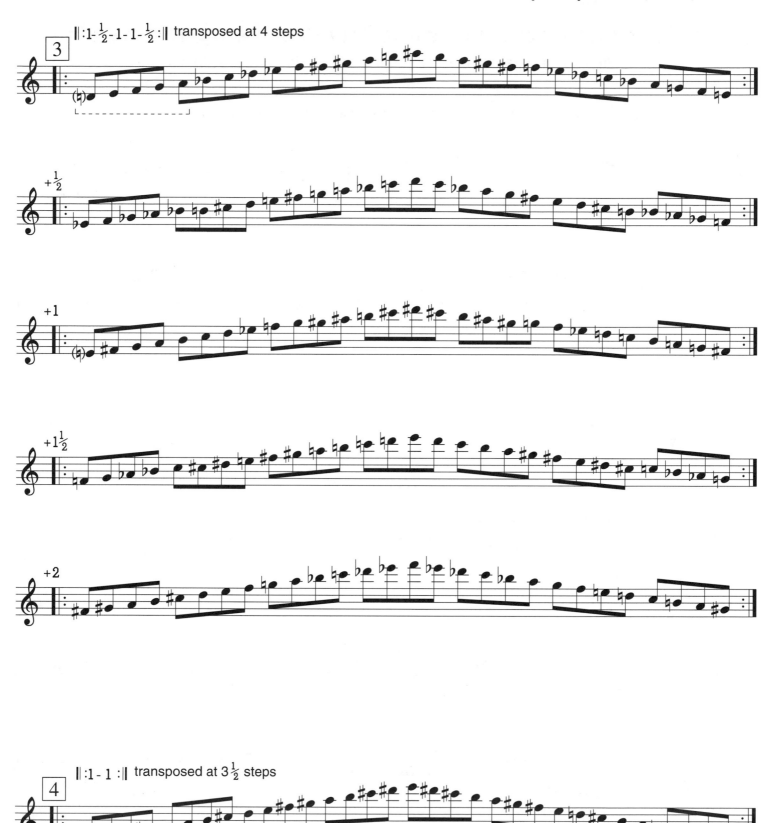

‖:1-½-1-1-½:‖ transposed at 4 steps

‖:1-1:‖ transposed at 3½ steps

40

IV. composed patterns (expanded)

patterns that expand on the concepts developed in exercises IIIa and IIIb

a. triads- structures derived from superimposing 3 different kinds of triads on one another

b. scales

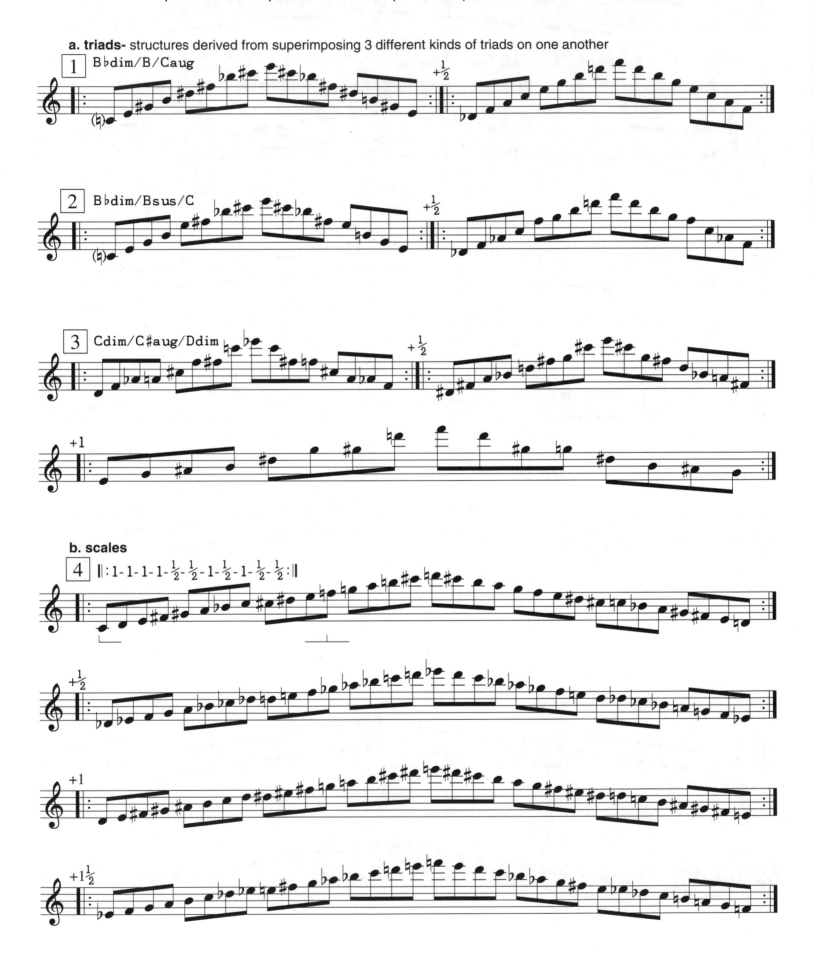

5   "freely" composed scale*

6

[mirror axis]
$1\frac{1}{2}$-1-1-1-1-$\frac{1}{2}$-1-$[\frac{1}{2}]$-1-$\frac{1}{2}$-1-1-1-1-$1\frac{1}{2}$ (see **Shepherd Of The Galaxis** on page 9)

7

* Freely-composed scales within a specific range, as in examples 5 and 6, are called "finite" scales.

V. chromatic transposition of fractals

Please note the difference between juxtaposition (V) and superimposition (previous exercises) of fractals. A versatile player-composer interchanges both principles constantly to create an interesting horizontal flow (see Etudes).

EXERCISES ADDENDUM

This section is designed to show you how to apply and practice the exercises in a creative way.

There are no phrasing, articulation or dynamic marks in this section. You should modify speed, articulation and dynamics freely, although a moderately fast jazz tempo with appropriate articulation works best. See the Performance Notes on page 7.

The roman numerals and brackets refer to specific exercises (pages 21- 43).

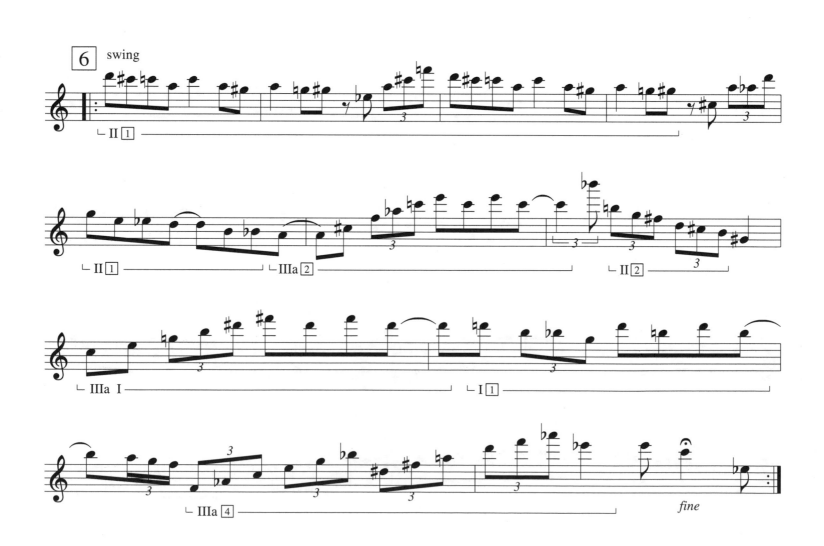

About Daniel Schnyder

Born in 1961 in Zurich, and now living in New York, Daniel Schnyder studied at the Conservatory of Winterthur, Switzerland; at Boston's Berklee College of Music and at the Banff Centre in Canada. Schnyder is known as a composer and as a performer (flute and saxophone) with a solid reputation in both the jazz and classical fields.

He has recorded over 16 CDs of his own music and has toured with such jazz artists as Hubert Laws, Lew Soloff, Ray Anderson, Kenny Drew, Jr., Marvin "Smitty" Smith and Victor Lewis. His orchestral works and chamber music have been performed in Europe, the Americas and Australia by such orchestras as the Atlanta Symphony, the Tonhallen Orchestra Zurich (**4th Symphony** initiated and commissioned by David Zinman), the NDR Big Band, the Opera of Bern, the Colleguim Musicum of Paul Sacher (**Viola Concerto**), National TV of Switzerland (**3rd Symphony**), the Bern Symphony (**Piano Concerto**), the Zürcher Kammerorchester (**Concerto for Flute, Percussion, and Strings**), the NDR Symphony, (**Concerto for Jazz Soloist(s) and Symphony Orchestra**, **Violin Concerto**, **Trumpet Concerto**, and **4th Symphony**), the Vienna Art Orchestra, the St. Paul Chamber Orchestra, the Swiss Youth Orchestra (**1st Symphony** under the direction of Maestro Andreas Delfs), various chamber music ensembles, classical soloists and jazz recording artists.

The early '90s marked the beginning of the ascent of Mr. Schnyder's career. In 1994, Daniel was invited as a composer in residence to the Barossa Music Festival, the leading chamber music festival in Australia. In 1995, he toured the continent with his quintet Nucleus, featuring

Kenny Drew, Jr., Michael Formanek, Michael Phillip Mossman and Victor Lewis. Schnyder's opera, based on William Shakespeare's "The Tempest," was commissioned by the Opera of Bern and premiered in June of 1996 under the direction of Hans Drewanz. In 1997, he toured Europe and Australia with his septet Tarantula, which featured some of New York's finest instrumentalists. That same year, his arrangement of Thelonious Monk's "Think Of One" was performed by the Chicago Sinfonietta and the T.S. Monk Sextet at the celebration of Thelonious Monk's 80th birthday. His arrangement and orchestration of Bizet's "Carmen Fantasy" was premiered by Marina Piccinini with the Milwaukee Symphony Orchestra in April, 1998. Subsequently the orchestra commissioned Schnyder to write **The Revelation of St. John**, a large scale work for chorus, symphony, organ and soloists that was premiered with great success in February 2001. At the present time, Mr. Schnyder is involved in a diverse array of musical endeavors. He frequently performs with his special chamber music project for saxophone and string quartet, "Zoom In," combining composition and improvisation, jazz and traditional chamber music. He appears as a soloist with orchestras playing his **Songbook** for Saxophone and Orchestra. He is a composer with Universal Edition's "Spectrum Series" and composer in residence with the Milwaukee Symphony Orchestra. Various prestigious organizations commission new Schnyder works in both the jazz and classical idioms.

Daniel Schnyder's work has been and continues to be extensively documented on recordings. "Strings For Holiday," produced and arranged by Schnyder and recorded in 1996, is dedicated to the great jazz singer Billie Holiday and features legendary jazz saxophonist Lee Konitz with string sextet and rhythm section. South African pianist Abdullah Ibrahim's "African Suite" and "African Symphony" were both arranged, orchestrated and produced by Schnyder. Schnyder's trio (with Kenny Drew, Jr., and David Taylor) has two recordings available entitled "Words Within Music" and "Jazz Meets Weill and Gershwin" featuring chamber music by Daniel and music by George Gershwin, Kurt Weill, J.S. Bach, Vivaldi and Wagner. The New York based new music group Absolute Ensemble's album "Absolution" was produced by Daniel and features his **Trombone Concerto**. The album received a Grammy nomination for Best Classical Small Ensemble Recording in 2002. Cuban born and New York based saxophonist Paquito d'Rivera's "Habanera" is a bold and innovative project arranged and produced by Schnyder that combines jazz and classical music. Please refer to the appended discography for a more comprehensive list of Schnyder's recorded work.

Mr. Schnyder has received numerous awards for his work including first prize at the 1996 International Trumpet Guild's Composition Contest, the Conrad and Ferdinand Meyer Prize, the Zolliker Kunstpries, awards for his chamber music by the International Flute Association (**Sailing**), the International Clarinet Association, the City of Zurich, Pro Helvetia, the National Art Council of Switzerland, the American Symphony League and Meet the Composer.

Mr. Schnyder gives master classes in composition and improvisation.

More information and short audio clips at http://www.danielschnyder.com and http://www.secondfloormusic.com.

Recordings

Nucleus (Enja 8068 2) all original jazz quintet compositions

Decoding The Message (Enja 6036 2) all original compositions scored for large mixed jazz ensemble

The City (Enja 6002 2) original four horn jazz arrangements in "avant garde" post bop style

Mythology (Enja 7003 2) original jazz compositions for three horns, string quartet, bass, and drums

Franco Ambrosetti: Music for Symphony and Jazz Band (Enja 6070 2) jazz standards and Daniel Schnyder originals arranged for large symphony orchestra and jazz sextet

Secret Cosmos (Enja 5055 2) chamber jazz compositions for six horns and double bass

Winds (Koch Schwann Records CD 31012H1) new original chamber music for wind instruments

Mythen (Koch Schwann Records 310170H1) new original chamber music

Daniel Schnyder / Michael Mossman Quintet: Granulat (Red Records 123240) featuring the original compositions of Daniel Schnyder and Michael Mossman

Tarantula (Enja 9302 2) all original compositions, many based on Weber's "Der Freischutz" scored for six horns and double bass, string quartet and saxophone, or large symphony orchestra and saxophone

David Jolley: Villanelle (Arabesque Z6678) features Schnyder's award-winning "Le Monde Minuscule" for solo French horn

Lee Konitz: Strings For Holiday (Enja 9304 2) tribute to Billie Holiday featuring Lee Konitz, arranged for string sextet, saxophone, bass, and drums by Daniel Schnyder

Abdullah Ibrahim: African Suite (Tiptoe 888 832 2) music of Abdullah Ibrahim arranged by Daniel Schnyder for large symphony orchestra, piano, bass, and drums

Abdullah Ibrahim: African Symphony (Enja 9410 2) music of Abdullah Ibrahim arranged by Daniel Schnyder for large symphony orchestra, piano, bass, and drums

Words Within Music (Enja 9369 2) featuring Daniel Schnyder, David Taylor and Kenny Drew, Jr.: chamber music and chamber jazz from Vivaldi to Bach, Wagner to Gershwin, plus new original compositions

Bernhard Rothlisberger: Who Nose (Gallo CD-9517) featuring "Who Nose" and "Clarinet Sonata"

Jazz Meets Weill and Gershwin (Koch Jazz 3-6969-2) played by David Taylor, Kenny Drew, Jr., and Daniel Schnyder

Eos Guitar Quartet: Quadra (DG 472 581-2) includes Schnyder's "Music For Four Guitars"

Songbook (CCnC 02322) Symphony Orchestra of Norrlands Opera directed by Kristjan Järvi, featuring Kenny Drew Jr. and Daniel Schnyder

Absolute Ensemble: Absolution (Enja 9394 2) Absolute Ensemble directed by Kristjan Järvi, featuring "Trombone Concerto"

Paquito D'Rivera: Habanera (Enja 9395 2) Paquito D'Rivera with the Absolute Ensemble directed by Kristjan Järvi, arranged and produced by Daniel Schnyder

Colossos Of Sound (Enja Nova) featuring Schnyder's "4th Symphony," "Violin Concerto" and "Trumpet Concerto"

Da Skale (TCB Records) featuring Daniel Schnyder/Kenny Drew, Jr. Quartet

Zoom In (Universal) featuring Daniel Schnyder and Strings (Carmina Quartet and James Haddad on percussion)

Compositions In Print

Other Second Floor Music publications by Daniel Schnyder

recorded on **Secret Cosmos**, Daniel Schnyder (Enja 5055):

Sailing (HL00841159) solo flute

Blues Variations (HL00000588) flute, tenor sax, trumpet, French horn, trombone, bass trombone, bass

Isabelle (HL00000592) flute, tenor sax, trumpet, French horn, trombone, bass trombone, bass

Secret Cosmos (HL00000596) flute, soprano sax, trumpet, French horn, trombone, bass trombone, bass

Septet No. 1 (HI00000598) flute/piccolo, soprano sax, trumpet, French horn, trombone, bass trombone, bass

Septet No. 2 (HL00000600) flute, soprano sax, trumpet, French horn, trombone, bass trombone, bass

Song For My Grandfather (HL00000602) flute, tenor sax, flugelhorn, French horn, trombone, bass trombone, bass

recorded on **Villanelle**, David Jolley (Arabesque Z6678):

Le Monde Minuscule (HL00841160) solo French horn

Second Floor Music products are distributed exclusively by the Hal Leonard Corp., available from your local music dealer (or order from Music Dispatch at 1-800-637-2852). More detailed information and RealAudio(TM) clips are available at www.secondfloormusic.com.

Other flute music by Daniel Schnyder

Flute Sonata (for flute and piano) Universal Edition (UE 70021)
Suite Provençale (9 pieces for 2 flutes) Universal Edition (UE 70022)
Concerto for flute, percussion and strings Universal Edition
Baroquelochness (for flute and piano/harpsichord and bassoon/cello ad lib.) Edition Kunzelmann/Peters
Melousine (for flute and piano, as played by the Ensemble Miroir) Edition Kunzelmann
Portrait Of Charlie Parker (flute and piano) Edition Kunzelmann/Peters)
Who Nose (flute and piano) Edition Kunzelmann/Peters
Trio For Flute, Piano and Violoncello (Bassoon) Edition Kunzelmann
Woodwind Quintet Edition Kunzelmann/Peters
Trio For Palladio (flute, cello and harpsichord) Edition Kunzelmann
Carmen Variations for solo flute and orchestra (Bizet/Schnyder) DANYMU
Little Songbook for Jazz soloist and Woodwind quintet DANYMU
Alone Together (for flute, clarinet, violin, viola, violoncello, bass, harp) Edition Kunzelmann
The Four Elements (for flute and piano) DANYMU

Publisher contact information:
Advance Music, Maieräckerstr. 18, 72108 Rottenburg, Germany. Tel.: 49 (0) 7472 - 1832,
website: www.advancemusic.com, email: mail@advancemusic.com
DANYMU, fax 1-917-507-8268; info@danielschnyder.com / www.danielschnyder.com
Edition Kunzelmann/Peters: order online at www.edition-peters.com or email irene@kunzelmann.com;
For rental call 1-718-416-7805 (Peters)
Universal Edition: email breneis@universaledition.com.

General information and questions: www.danielschnyder.com

http://www.secondfloormusic.com

USE OUR WEB SITE TO:

- **hear RealAudio™ clips of each chart**

- **find charts for your group's exact instrumentation**

- **click on any of the fields under SEARCH BY to search for charts. Use the drop-down boxes to fill in the form. *Fill in just the information you're looking for*, like the group size or the level of difficulty you want. Our search engine will compile a list of charts that fit. Click on a title to see details and get the RealAudio icon.**

- **You can also search for charts recorded by some of the great musicians we publish, or the specific instrumentation of your combo.**

- **Try looking for a chart by tempo and group size. Or use the drop-down list under Recording Leader or Recording Title to see what artists have recorded these charts.**

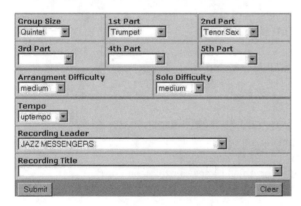

The completed form shown here will display all uptempo quintet charts, medium difficulty, that were recorded by the Jazz Messengers and have a trumpet and tenor sax front line. Select

a title from the results screen and you can hear a short audio clip while you read detailed information about the arrangement, the solo section, the composer and even the recording.

- **browse by composer**

- **browse by composition title**

- **browse by group size: just pick your group size from the drop-down box in the SEARCH BY page**

- **click on a title to see a brief description, including instrumentation, tempo, style, form, solo changes and level of difficulty**

- **click on the RealAudio icon to hear the opening melody**

- **chart descriptions also include brief biographies of our composers**

- **e-mail comments and questions to our staff**

- **request a complete printed catalog**

- **from the HOW TO ORDER page, link to online music dealers and the Hal Leonard Corporation**

- **order our charts from your local music dealer, or order by phone from Music Dispatch at 1-800-637-2852.**

- Use your web browser to visit **http: // www.secondfloormusic.com.** Jazz is our passion—let us show you why!